Chew On This

Homemade
Dog Treat Recipes

Published by

Chew On This Publishing, LLC

Contents

Introduction

I started making my own dog treats shortly after I left my corporate job and began working from home. Just like my home cooked meals for Jim and myself, the homemade treats for my dogs are free of artificial flavors, chemicals, and preservatives. I love that I know exactly what I am feeding my dogs and they love the treats!

When I started to share some of the recipes on my blog: "Keep Your Paws on the Road," I had a lot of people tell me they loved making them. Out of this came the idea to compile the recipes into a cookbook to make it available for more dog lovers.

I hope you will enjoy making these treats for your dog(s).
I know your dog(s) will love them!

Sincerely,
Birgit Walker

A Few Words about
Ingredients

The beauty about making your own dog treats is that you choose your ingredients based on your personal preference and, if needed, can adjust them according to your dog's food sensitivities.

Many of the recipes in the book use whole wheat. If you have a dog with a wheat allergy, you can easily substitute with other flours. There are a lot of other flour choices and any will work. Keep in mind that depending on the type of flour you use, you may need to adjust the amount of water or liquid used to make the batter. This is why I recommend you always add the liquid (water) slowly so you can get the right consistency for your dough.

When a recipe calls for peanut butter, please be sure to select unsalted natural peanut butter. NEVER use sugar-free or lite peanut butter, as it contains artificial sweeteners that are toxic for your dog!

Some of the recipes use eggs. If your dog does not tolerate eggs in his diet, you can substitute each egg with one banana or three tablespoons of unsweetened applesauce.

Always store your homemade treats in airtight containers in your refrigerator or freezer. Use them within a few weeks. Remember, there are no preservatives in these treats.

Wheat Biscuits

Directions:

Preheat oven to 350° F (176° C)

Combine the wheat flour, powdered dry milk, salt and brown sugar into large bowl.

Cut in the melted butter until mealy.

Mix in the beaten egg.

Add the ice water slowly until mixture forms a doughball.

Roll out dough about 1/4" thick and cut into desired shapes.

Arrange biscuits greased cookie sheet and bake for about 20-30 minutes.

Let them cool off completely before you feed them!

Store in airtight container for up to 3 weeks in fridge or freeze.

Ingredients:

2 ½ cups wheat flour

½ cup powdered dry milk

½ teaspoon salt

1 teaspoon brown sugar

6 tablespoons melted butter

1 egg, beaten

½ cup ice water

Wheat Germ Treats

Directions:

Preheat oven to 350° F (176° C)

Combine the wheat germ, baby food and water into large bowl.

Dough should be thick and crumbly.

Lightly dust a surface with wheat flour and roll out the dough - about 1/4" thick.

Cut into desired shapes.

Arrange treats on lined cookie sheet and bake for about 15-20 minutes.

You want the treats to be firm and crisp.

Always allow treats to completely cool, before feeding.

Store in airtight container in your fridge for up to 2 weeks or freeze them.

Ingredients:

2 cups wheat germ

3 jars of chicken and broth organic baby food (2.5 oz jars)

2 tablespoons of water

PB & Oat Biscuits

🐾🐾🐾🐾🐾

Directions:

Preheat oven to 350° F (176° C)

Combine all ingredients into large bowl.

Knead dough into ball, add more water or broth if the dough is to dry.

Lightly dust a surface with wheat flour and roll out the dough - about 1/4" thick.

Cut into desired shapes.

Arrange treats on a greased cookie sheet and bake for 30 minutes.

You want the treats to be hard and crunchy.

Let treats cool completely, before you feed them!

Store in airtight container for up to 2 weeks in your fridge, or freeze them.

Ingredients:

2 cups whole wheat flour

½ cup oats

1 egg

¼ cup natural peanut butter

½ cup beef broth

Cheesy Biscuits

Directions:

Preheat oven to 350° F (176° C)

Heat chicken broth until warm, then add remaining ingredients.

Knead dough until smooth.

Roll dough to ½ inch and use cookie cutters to make shaped cookies.

Arrange on lined cookie sheet.

Bake for 30 minutes

Let treats cool off completely, before you feed them!

Store in your fridge for up to 2 weeks or freeze them.

Ingredients:

2 ½ cups of oats

¼ cup shredded cheese

¼ cup bacon bits

½ cup chicken broth

1 egg

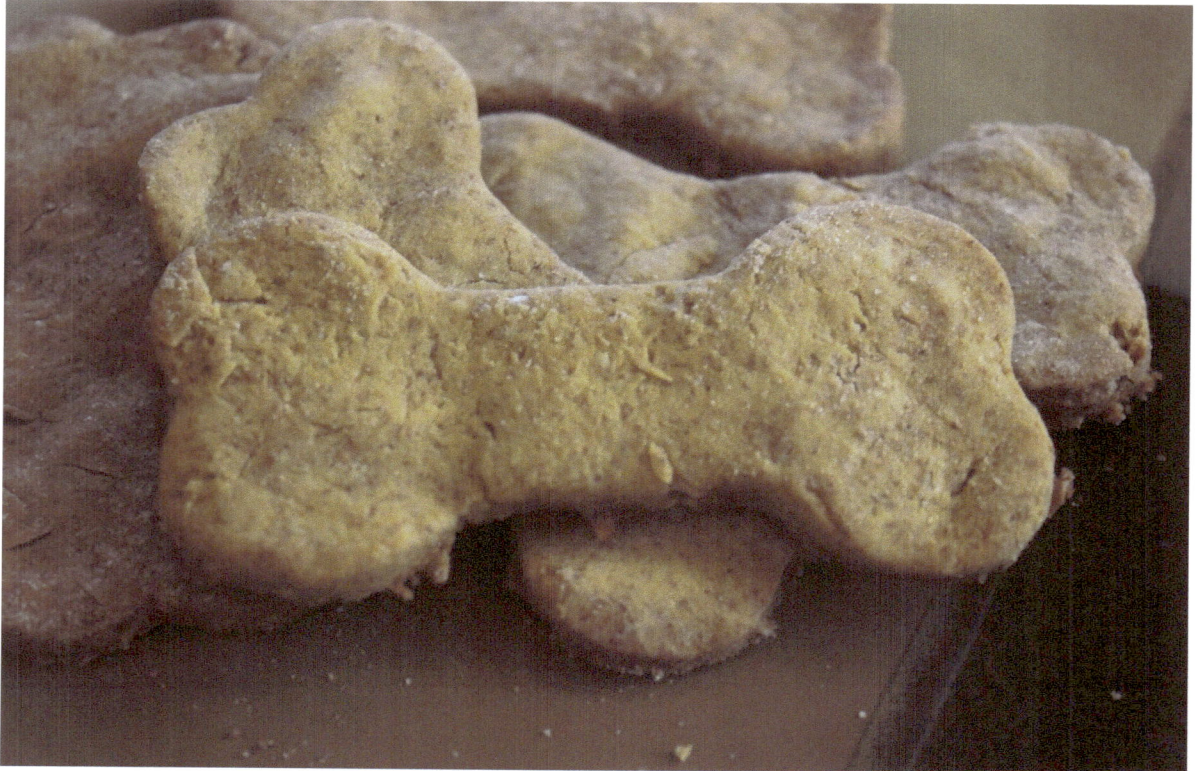

Pumpkin Cookies

Directions:

Preheat oven to 350° F (175° C)

Combine all ingredients in a large bowl. Add the water slowly until dough forms a ball.

Roll dough to ¼ inch on floured surface, use cookie cutters to cut into desired shaped cookies

Arrange on greased cookie sheet.

Bake for 20-30 minutes until golden brown.

Let treats cool completely, before you feed them!

Store in airtight container for 2 weeks in fridge or freeze.

Ingredients:

1 ½ cup oat flour

1 ½ cup brown rice flour

½ cup canned pumpkin

1 egg

2 tablespoons molasses

1 tablespoon honey

water as needed

Fresh Breath Patties

Directions:

Preheat oven to 350° F (175° C)

Mix parsley, carrots, mint, cheese and oil in large bowl. Add the flour and then add water slowly to make a moist dough.

Knead dough until smooth. About 5 minutes.

Dust your hands with flour and form small patties from the dough.

Arrange patties on lined cookie sheet.

Bake for 20 minutes until lightly browned.

Let treats cool completely, before you feed them!

Store in airtight container for up to 1 week in your fridge or freeze them to store for up to 3 weeks.

Ingredients:

2 cups of brown rice flour

½ cup of finely shredded carrots

1 cup of fresh shredded parsley

2 tablespoons of finely chopped dried mint

¼ cup shredded cheese

2 tablespoons avocado oil

water as needed

15

Applesauce Cookies

🐾🐾🐾🐾🐾

Directions:

Preheat oven to 350° F (176° C)

Combine all ingredients in a bowl and mix thoroughly.

Knead dough until smooth.

Roll dough to ¼ inch on floured surface.

Use cookie cutters to make shaped cookies, or make small dough balls.

Arrange cookies on lined cookie sheet.

Bake for 20-30 minutes until lightly browned.

Let treats cool completely, before you feed them!

Store in airtight container for up to 2 weeks.

Ingredients:

2 cups of oats

3 cups of whole wheat flour

1 cup natural peanut butter

1 cup unsweetened apple sauce

¼ cup coconut oil

1 teaspoon of baking powder

Blue Oatmeal Cookies

🐾🐾🐾🐾🐾

Directions:

Preheat oven to 350° F (176° C)

In food processor or coffee grinder, turn oats into oatmeal powder and grind flaxseed if necessary.

Puree the blueberries.

Combine dry ingredients and then fold in the yogurt and blueberry puree. Add a little water to create a smooth dough.

Spoon dough into hands and form small dough balls. Shape into cookies.

Arrange cookies on greased cookie sheet.

Bake for 20 minutes, then flip and bake additional 10 minutes.

Let treats cool completely, before you feed them to your dogs!

Ingredients:

1 cup of oats

1 cup flaxseed

1 cup of blueberries

2 cups of whole wheat flour

½ cup plain yogurt

water as needed

19

Spinach & Rice Cakes

🐾🐾🐾🐾🐾

Directions:

Preheat oven to 350° F (176° C)

In food processor, turn oats into a coarse meal.

Combine all ingredients in bowl and mix well. Add additional broth, as needed, to create a smooth dough.

Roll dough to ¼ inch on floured surface. Use cookie cutters to make shaped cookies, or make small dough balls.

Arrange cookies on greased cookie sheet. Or use a fork to flatten dough balls.

Bake for 15-25 minutes until lightly browned.

Let treats cool completely, before you feed them!

Store in airtight container for 1 week in your fridge or freeze.

Ingredients:

2 cups of brown rice uncooked

2 cups oats

½ cup of chicken broth

1 cup of whole wheat flour

½ cup unsweetened apple sauce

1 can of spinach (drained)

Thanksgiving Treats

Directions:

Preheat oven to 375° F (200° C)

In food processor, puree raw carrot.

Cook and mash sweet potatoes. Cook and drain ground turkey.

Combine all ingredients in bowl and mix well to form dough.

Roll dough to ¼ inch on floured surface, use cookie cutters to make shaped cookies, or make small dough balls by hand.

Arrange cookies on greased cookie sheet. (Use a fork to flatten dough balls.)

Bake for 25-35 minutes until lightly browned.

Let treats cool completely, before you feed them to your dog!

Store in airtight container in fridge for few days or freeze.

Ingredients:

1 ½ cups oat flour

1 ½ cups brown rice flour

½ cup ground turkey

1 large carrot

2 sweet potatoes

2 eggs

2 tablespoon honey

Green Cheese Cookies

Directions:

Thaw out and drain spinach.

Preheat oven to 350° F (176° C)

Combine all ingredients in bowl and mix well. Add the water slowly, as needed, to create a sticky dough.

With about a tablespoon of dough, make dough balls. You can make smaller cookies for small dogs or larger treats for bigger dogs.

Arrange treats on greased cookie sheet.

Bake for 20-30 minutes until lightly browned.

Let treats cool completely, before you feed them!

Store in airtight container for 1 week in your fridge or freeze.

Ingredients:

1 cup frozen spinach

1 cup oatmeal

1 cup mozzarella cheese

1 cup of brown rice flour

1 tablespoon coconut oil

water as needed

Hamburger Cookies

Directions:

Preheat oven to 350° F (176° C)

Cook and drain ground beef.

Combine all ingredients, adding water slowly, to form dough.

Spoon out dough and form small hamburger patties.

Arrange on greased cookie sheet.

Bake for 20-30 minutes until lightly browned. Flip halfway through baking time.

Let treats cool completely, before you feed them!

Store in airtight container for 2 days in fridge or freeze.

Ingredients:

1 ½ cups potato flour

1 ½ cups oatmeal

½ cup mild cheddar cheese

½ cup lean ground beef

1 egg

6 oz can tomato paste

water as needed

Turkey Bakes

Directions:

Preheat oven to 375° F (200° C)

Cook and drain ground turkey

Combine all ingredients, adding water slowly, to form dough

Roll dough to ¼ inch on floured surface. Use cookie cutters to cut into desired shaped cookies.

Arrange on greased cookie sheet.

Bake for 20-30 minutes until lightly browned. Flip halfway through baking time.

Let treats cool completely, before you feed them!

Store in airtight container for 2 days in fridge or freeze.

Ingredients:

1 ½ cups oat flour

1 ¼ cups brown rice flour

½ cup oat bran

½ cup ground turkey

1 egg

2 tablespoons tomato paste

1 tablespoon molasses

water as needed

Veggie Rice Cakes

Ingredients:

Directions:

Preheat oven to 350° F (175° C)

Mix parsley, carrots, mint, cheese, rice, and oil in large bowl.

Add water, as needed, to make a moist dough.

Form small balls from the dough, using your hands.

Arrange balls on lined cookie sheet. Use a fork to flatten them slightly.

Bake for 15 minutes until lightly browned.

Let treats cool completely, before you feed them!

Store in airtight container for up to 1 week in fridge or freeze them to store for up to 3 weeks.

2 cups of cooked brown rice

½ cup of shredded carrots

1 cup of shredded parsley

2 tablespoons of finely chopped dried mint

¼ cup shredded cheese

2 tablespoons avocado oil

water as needed

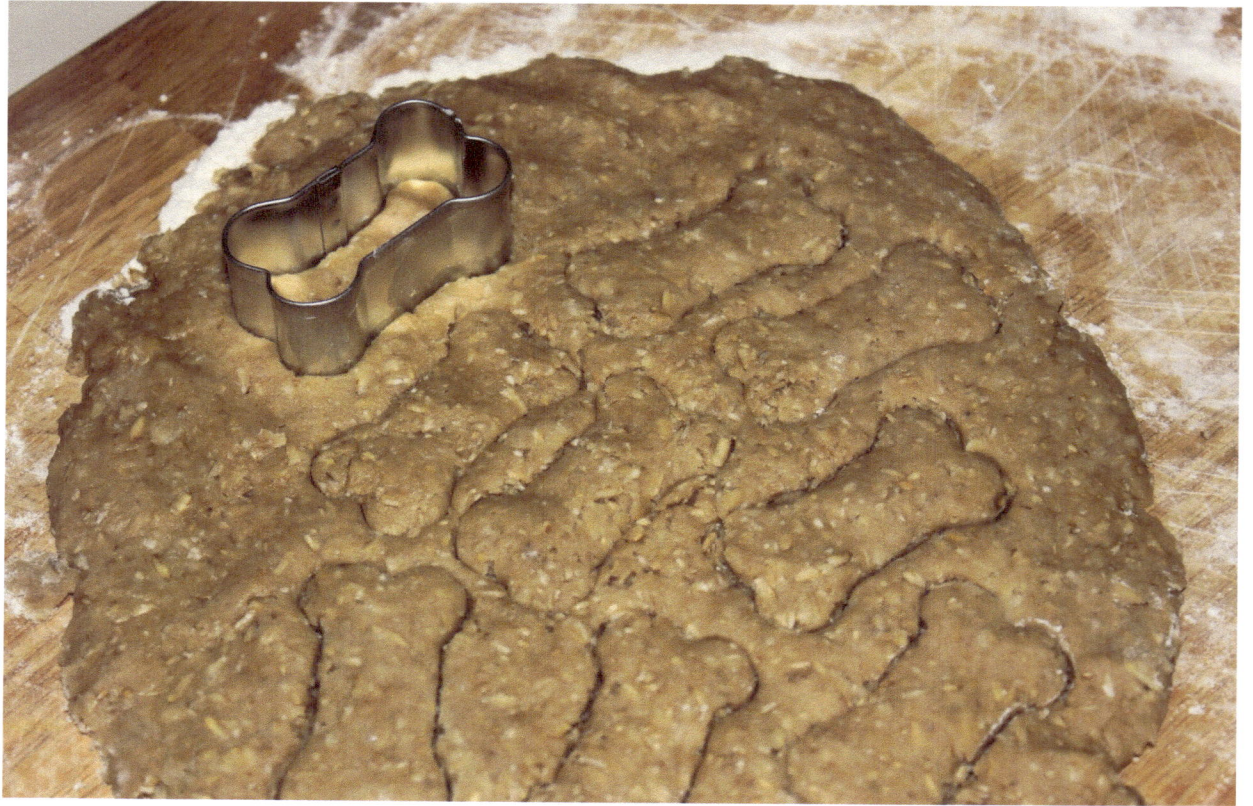

Crispy Apple Treats

Directions:

Preheat oven to 350° F (175° C)

Combine all ingredients. Add a little water slowly, to form dough.

Roll dough to ¼ inch on floured surface. Use cookie cutters to cut into desired shaped cookies.

Arrange on greased cookie sheet.

Bake for 20-25 minutes until golden brown.

Let treats cool completely, before you feed them!

Store in airtight container for 2 weeks in fridge or freeze.

Ingredients:

1 ½ cup oat flour

1 ½ cup brown rice flour

1 cup unsweetened apple sauce

½ cup rolled oats

1 egg

1 tablespoon honey

water as needed

PB & Pumpkin Bites

Directions:

Preheat oven to 350° F (175° C)

Mix eggs, canned pumpkin, and peanut butter in a large bowl until smooth.

Add flour to make a dry, stiff dough. Add water if needed to form dough ball.

Roll dough to ¼ inch on floured surface. Use cookie cutters to cut into desired shaped cookies. Or use hands to form small cookie patties.

Arrange treats on a greased cookie sheet.

Bake for 20-25 minutes. Flip cookies half way through the baking time.

Let treats cool completely, before you feed them!

Store in your fridge in airtight container for 1 week in fridge or freeze.

Ingredients:

2 ½ cups brown rice flour

¼ cup natural peanut butter

½ cup canned pumpkin

2 eggs

water as needed

35

No-bake PB Balls

🐾🐾🐾🐾🐾

Directions:

Melt coconut oil and combine with peanut butter until smooth.

Add oatmeal gradually until the dough is thick

Spoon into hands and form small balls. Adjust size to your dogs size.

Line cookie sheet with parchment paper and arrange dough balls onto sheet.

Place in refrigerator for at least one hour to let them settle.

Feed when ready.

Store in your fridge in airtight container for 1 week or freeze.

Ingredients:

3 cups oatmeal

1 cup natural peanut butter

¼ cup coconut oil

Pill Pockets

Directions:

Liquefy coconut oil and combine with peanut butter until smooth.

Use food processor to make oatmeal into flour.

Spoon into floured hands and form small balls. Adjust size to your dogs size.

Line cookie sheet with parchment paper and arrange dough balls onto sheet. Use the handle of a wooden spoon to make small indentation for the pill.

Place in refrigerator for at least one hour to let them settle.

Use when needed. Place pill inside pill pocket and squeeze dough to en-capsule medication.

Store in your fridge in airtight container for 1 week or freeze.

Ingredients:

½ cup peanut butter

½ cup oatmeal

½ cup coconut oil

Healthy Truffles

Directions:

Liquefy coconut oil and mix all ingredients, except the oats, in a large bowl.

Use spoon-full of dough to make small dough balls and roll them into oats.

Place in refrigerator for at least one hour to let them settle.

Feed when ready.

Store in your fridge in airtight container for few days.

Ingredients:

½ cup oatmeal

¼ cup canned pumpkin

½ cup natural peanut butter

2 tablespoons coconut oil

¼ cup of oats (to roll into)

41

PB & Banana Bones

🐾🐾🐾🐾🐾

Directions:

Puree bananas in food processor.

Mix all ingredients in a large bowl.

Use spoon to fill hollow soup bones or dog chew stuffers.

Place in freezer for several hours or overnight.

Feed when ready.

Ingredients:

2 ripe bananas

½ cup natural peanut butter

1 tablespoon honey

½ cup plain yogurt

Pupsicles

Ingredients:

2 ripe bananas

½ cup natural peanut butter

1 cup plain yogurt

Directions:

Puree the bananas and mix with peanut butter and yogurt.

Use spoon to fill into ice cup tray or small cupcake forms.

Place in freezer for several hours or overnight.

Feed when ready.

Pumpkinsicles

Directions:

Mix all ingredients in a large bowl.

Use spoon to fill paper cups or ice cube trays

Stick a dog bone treat halfway into each cup center.

Place in freezer for several hours or overnight.

Feed when ready.

Ingredients:

2 cups canned pumpkin

½ cup natural peanut butter

1 cup plain yogurt

Applesicles

Directions:

Peel the apple and remove the core. Use food processor to chop.

Mix apple with yogurt and coconut oil in a medium size bowl.

Pour into ice cube trays or silicon molds.

Freeze for several hours or overnight.

Feed when ready.

Ingredients:

1 large apple

½ cup plain yogurt

1 tablespoon coconut oil

Fresh-Breathsicles

Directions:

Use silicon molds or ice cube trays and fill them half way with chicken broth. Place in freezer for 2 hours.

Use food processor to finely chop parsley.

Mix peanut butter, coconut oil and parsley in a medium size bowl. You may need to liquefy the coconut oil in the microwave if it is hard.

Add mixture over the frozen chicken broth in ice cube trays or silicon molds.

Freeze for several hours or overnight.

Feed when ready.

Ingredients:

½ cup chicken broth

½ cup natural peanut butter

1 tablespoon coconut oil

¼ cup parsley

Honey & Berry Frozens

Directions:

Use food processor to puree blueberries.

Mix yogurt, honey and blueberries in a medium size bowl.

Poor into ice cube trays or silicon molds.

Freeze for several hours until solid.

Feed when ready. (Careful where your dog eats these. They can stain carpets when the treats melt!)

Ingredients:

1 cup blueberries

1 cup plain yogurt

2 tablespoons honey

My Own Dog Treat Recipes

Directions:

Ingredients:

_____

Directions:

Ingredients:

_____

🐾🐾🐾🐾🐾

Directions:

Ingredients:

_____

Directions:

Ingredients:

_____

🐾🐾🐾🐾🐾

Directions:

Ingredients:

_____

Directions:

Ingredients:

_____

🐾🐾🐾🐾🐾

Ingredients:

Directions:

Also by Birgit Walker

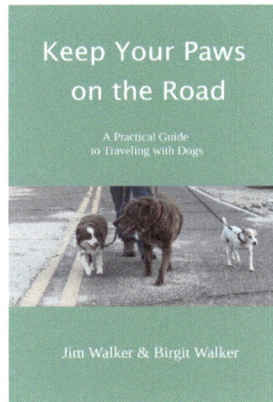

Keep Your Paws on the Road - A Practical Guide to Traveling with Dogs combines Birgit's love for travel with her husband's expertise in dog training. Their favorite dog adventures include paddle boarding in Montana, biking in Idaho, walking the beaches of California and hiking in Oregon.

When she isn't planning new dog-friendly adventures, you can find Birgit writing on her blog Keep Your Paws on the Road, a site that shares dog treat recipes, dog training tips, and reviews dog-friendly travel. You can follow Birgit and Jim on their website, Modern Canine Services or connect with Birgit in her lively Facebook Group.

Come to ModernCanineServices.com for links to the blog, Facebook Group and YouTube Channel!

www.ingramcontent.com/pod-product-compliance
Lightning Source LLC
Chambersburg PA
CBHW060811090426
42737CB00002B/31